In Scotland

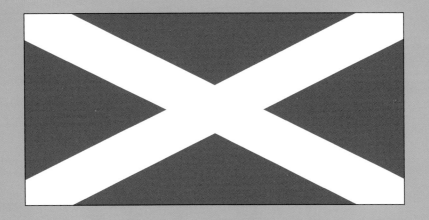

written by **Judy Zocchi** illustrated by **Neale Brodie**

dingles & company New Jersey

To my love, DSZ

First printing

PUBLISHED BY dingles&company
P.O. Box 508 • Sea Girt, New Jersey • 08750
WEBSITE: www.dingles.com • E-MAIL: info@dingles.com

Library of Congress Catalog Card No.: 2004094740
ISBN: 1-59646-012-1

Printed in the United States of America

ART DIRECTION & DESIGN BY Barbie Lambert
ENGLISH EDITED BY Andrea Curley
RESEARCH AND ADDITIONAL COPY WRITTEN BY Robert Neal Kanner
EDUCATIONAL CONSULTANT Bridget Riley Turnbach
ASSISTANT DESIGNER Theresa Makani
PRE-PRESS BY Pixel Graphics

The Global Adventures series takes children on an around-the-world exploration of a variety of fascinating countries. The series examines each country's history and physical features as well as its most popular customs, activities, and foods.

Global Adventures

Judy Zocchi

is the author of the Global Adventures, Holiday Happenings, Click & Squeak's Computer Basics, and Paulie and Sasha series. She is a writer and lyricist who holds a bachelor's degree in fine arts/theater from Mount Saint Mary's College and a master's degree in educational theater from New York University. She lives in Manasquan, New Jersey, with her husband, David.

Neale Brodie

is a freelance illustrator who lives in Brighton, England, with his wife and young daughter. He is a self-taught artist, having received no formal education in illustration. As well as illustrating a number of children's books, he has worked as an animator in the computer games industry.

In Scotland
a CROFT is a farm.

A croft is a small field or pasture that the owner of a large estate rents to someone to farm.

ENGLISH is what people speak.

Almost all Scots speak Standard Scottish English, which is basically standard English spoken with a Scottish accent.

It's cold. Let's go for a short walk.
Okay. Come on, girl.

SHETLAND SHEEP
produce soft wool.

These sheep come from the Shetland Islands, north of the mainland. Their wool is soft, yet strong and durable. It comes in a wide variety of shades, from the whitest of whites to the darkest black.

A **PUFFIN** has a triangular beak.

This is one of the most numerous of Scotland's seabirds. It has a parrotlike beak, bright orange legs, and small wings that beat rapidly.

In Scotland GOLF was invented.

This game was invented on the east coast of Scotland and was played as early as the 14th century. Players use golf clubs to hit a tiny ball around a golf course with many obstacles and eventually drop the ball into a tiny hole. The town of Saint Andrews is home to what is considered to be the oldest golf course.

HAGGIS is a favorite dish.

This dish is made from the organs of a sheep or calf. The organs are chopped up, mixed with oatmeal and seasonings, and then boiled in a sheep's lining, like a large sausage.

Many dance the
HIGHLAND FLING.

This dance was created in the 1700s as a victory dance performed by soldiers when they won a battle or a war. The fling is a leg kick that is the dance step.

HERRING

is a local fish.

Herring fishing is an important industry for Scotland. The small silver-colored fish are caught in the shallow waters off the coast of Scotland.

In Scotland most families have a TARTAN.

A tartan is a checkered pattern woven into a material such as a woolen cloth. In the past, a weaver created the distinctive pattern, which was then used by the chief or head of the family or clan.

KILTS are males' traditional dress.

Kilts are knee-length skirts with pleats that are worn by men and boys as formal dress for special occasions, such as parades or weddings.

The CABER TOSS is dangerous.

This is a traditional Scottish sport in which a player throws a large wooden pole called a caber into the air. The caber must turn end over end and point in a certain direction when it lands. Players lose points when the throw is less than perfect.

Tourists hunt Nessie in LOCH NESS.

Loch (or lake) Ness is a large lake—23 miles long, a mile wide, and about 600 feet deep. Some people believe it is the home of a prehistoric sea serpent called Nessie.

Scottish culture is fun to learn.

CROFT

ENGLISH

SHETLAND SHEEP

PUFFIN

GOLF

HAGGIS
(HAG-is)

HIGHLAND FLING

HERRING

TARTAN
(TAR-tn)

KILTS

CABER TOSS
(KAY-ber)

LOCH NESS
(lohk)

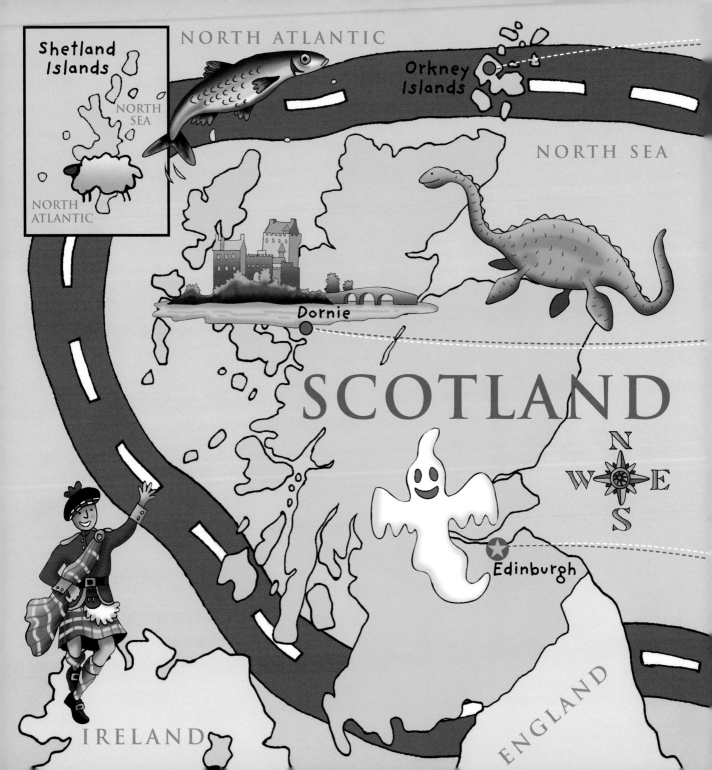

NORTH ATLANTIC

Shetland Islands

NORTH SEA

NORTH ATLANTIC

Orkney Islands

NORTH SEA

Dornie

SCOTLAND

N
W E
S

Edinburgh

IRELAND

ENGLAND

Orkney Islands: Some people believe that these fog-covered islands were home to a race of sorcerers called Finfolk. There are also documented tales of mermaid sightings here.

Dornie: You can visit Filean Donan Castle here in the Highlands. It was built in 1220 as the first line of defense against the Vikings.

Edinburgh: Many people died in the black plague of the seventeenth century, and some believe that their ghosts may walk the underground streets in the city.

See what you can discover at every turn!

OFFICIAL NAME:
Scotland
(United Kingdom of Great Britain
and Northern Ireland)

CAPITAL CITY:
Edinburgh

CURRENCY:
British pound

MAJOR LANGUAGES:
English, Gaelic, Scots

BORDERS:
North Sea, England, Irish Sea,
Atlantic Ocean

CONTINENT: Europe

ABOUT SCOTLAND

Two warring Celtic tribes, the Picts and the Scots, were the early inhabitants of the region. The Romans conquered the area in 82 C.E. and named it Caledonia. The country was established when the tribes were united under one kingdom called Dal Riada in 843 by Kenneth McAlpin, king of the Scots. The English and Scots battled over the area for many centuries. Scotland formally united with England in 1707 to form Great Britain. Soon after, poor treatment by English monarchs resulted in two big uprisings. The English put down the rebellions, but that caused many Scots to leave the country. Today Scotland is one of four nations that form the United Kingdom of Great Britain and Northern Ireland. (The others are England, Wales, and Northern Ireland.) In 1999 Scotland elected its own parliament, or governing body, for the first time in 300 years. Scotch whiskey production, oil, gas, and electronics are among the main industries in Scotland.

UNDERSTANDING AND CELEBRATING CULTURAL DIFFERENCES

- What do you have in common with children from Scotland?
- What things do you do differently from the children in Scotland?
- What is your favorite new thing you learned about Scotland?
- What unique thing about your culture would you like to share?

TRAVELING THROUGH SCOTLAND

- Which sea does the capital of Scotland, Edinburgh, border?
- Can you name the islands directly to the north of Scotland?
- In which direction would you be traveling if you went from Edinburgh to Glasgow?
- If you travel by boat through the North Channel along Scotland's coast, in which cities would you stop?

TRY SOMETHING NEW...

Scottish children love to make up rhymes about the games they play. Together with your friends, make up rhymes to help explain the games you play to someone who doesn't know how to play them.